When God Said Yes

A Woman's Journey from Rejection to Total Trust in
God's Timing For Love

NIKKI CARPENTER

Dedication

To all the women waiting for their "When God Said Yes"
moment, this is for you.

Contents

Acknowledgments

To my husband Steve. You are the reason why this book exists. Your unexpected love still surprises me. A couple of forevers, please. To my family: Thank you for always believing in me. To my Lord & Savior, Jesus Christ: In you I live, move, and have my very being. Thank you for making all things possible. I love you all. Deeply.

Introduction

I never liked the singles ministry. For some reason it seemed like the underlying purpose was for singles to find their soulmate, or just discuss the fact that they were single and lonely. Don't get me wrong—at one point in my life I was perfectly okay with such a setting.

However, I knew I was growing when I stopped attending a singles group because all they talked about was marriage. Clearly we were all single, but our singleness wasn't meant to be lived in vain. Was I the only Christian who read the following scripture and took it to heart?

There is a difference between a wife and a virgin. The unmarried woman careth for the things of the Lord, that she may be holy both in body and in spirit.

1 Corinthians 7:34

After years and years of doing things the wrong way, my spirit yearned for truth. I'd been doing things wrong from the beginning. God bless my heart, I try to take blame when I should, but it wasn't entirely my fault.

Growing up in the African-American church, I now realize how much of an unhealthy emphasis we've placed on marriage. Ninety percent of our conversations consisted of discussing our "Boaz," wedding colors, baby names, etc. I was even encouraged by leaders of my church to plan my wedding. Keep in mind I wasn't dating anyone, was only 21 years old, and hadn't finished college. There was so much more I could have been doing, besides planning a wedding that wouldn't take place in my life until nine years later.

Our idolization of marriage has been detrimental to some singles and even married folks. As a single woman who once experienced pressure from the church to be married, sometimes I felt inadequate. I also felt secluded, because there were plenty of sermons and events for the married folks, but for the singles? Not so much. And since the single person has pretty much idolized marriage, they'll more than likely go into their marriage expecting it to be their "cure" for everything. What a letdown it is the moment you discover your spouse can't completely make you whole. They are simply human. That role belongs to Christ alone.

I've read my share of Christian books for singles. They did nothing for me except increase my desire for marriage, which at the time wasn't beneficial for my growth as a single woman, who should have been caring about the things of the Lord. It wasn't long before I completely stopped purchasing these books. Years later I came across *Lady in Waiting: Becoming God's Best While Waiting for Mr. Right* by Jackie Kendall and Debbie Jones. A friend and I dissected this book together. It literally changed our lives. Finally, someone spoke on how to guard your heart as a single woman desiring marriage. I believe God used them to write *Lady in Waiting*. They were saying what I needed to hear, for years. I believed every single woman needed to read this book, so soon I began to have Twitter chats/discussions about it. I even wrote about it on my blog, NikkiAndTheCity.com. It was a new movement that totally revolutionized my thought process about being a single woman in the church. It liberated me.

After I got engaged, the pieces came together and it all made sense. Why had I ever doubted God's plan for me? Why did I let my single status cause me to deal with rejection and loneliness? Why did I want to live up to society's standard of success instead of God's standard of holiness?

To everything there is a season, and a time to every purpose under the heaven.

Ecclesiastes 3:1

It wasn't easy, but I now know it was totally worth the wait. Journey with me, as I take you through the lessons and seasons leading up to when God said yes.

Chapter 1:
#1 Reject

At 22, I experienced my first heartbreak.

We met when I was 16. I remember it like it was yesterday when he first asked me for my phone number. At the time, I wasn't allowed to talk on the phone with boys, so I took his number instead. He was the son of a preacher, and since my mother was a minister we had something in common. I loved the way he respected me. It was rare for a guy in high school not to be persuasive or hint at sex, but he never did. This is why I considered him a friend first. I even came to see him off for his senior prom and privately hinted about how I wished he was taking me. He went away to college in a nearby state and started dating a girl he met at school. Our friendship remained, but there was always a slight crush for each other lingering in the back of our minds.

I can't pinpoint when the slight crush became a major crush, but I do remember us beginning to talk on the phone every day. I was starting to fall for him, but there was one major problem: he had a girlfriend. I still remember our conversation when he informed me he'd broken up with her. I tried to pretend like it wasn't a big deal, but on the inside I was doing cartwheels. After years of something always being in the way, it was finally our moment.

I knew he was the one for me. My mom always knew when he was coming home for a visit, because my hair and eyebrows would be on point! One time I purchased a bottle of my favorite perfume at the time, Clinique Happy, and literally didn't open it until the day he came home. I was always saving my best for him. We talked every day, sometimes all night long. I did visit him on campus a few times, but for the most part I was always anxiously waiting for him to come home.

The first time he told me he loved me before we got off the phone, I was in utter shock. I didn't say it back at first, because my stepfather was nearby. Saying "I love you" to him for others to hear meant it was real. Especially if "others" are your parents. However, I did love him, and wasn't going to let him get off the phone without knowing it, so I said it back. My stepfather's reaction was humorous and it was officially known to the family that Nikki was in love. He soon became a household name and my family took a liking to him. I knew it was real the time I was out of town in Atlanta, and he was back home in Chicago at my little brother's birthday party, without me. Things were getting real. We continued to get closer and one day went window shopping for a ring. That experience was breathtaking for me. He was the first guy to ever tell me he loved me, and actually back it up with the possibility of putting a ring on my finger.

As he asked me to show him what style of ring I liked the most, he must have picked up on my uncertainty. It's as if my feet were stuck and I had a loss for words, which never happens to me. Although I was quiet for a moment, a million thoughts were going through my mind: "He wanted me? He wanted to marry me? He was going to buy *me* a ring? Is this real?" I slowly made my way through the store and apprehensively pointed out rings I adored. I couldn't believe this was happening. He was going to ask me to marry him and we would be together forever.

It never happened. He went on an international mission trip with his church on campus. I knew something was off when he failed to call me as soon as he returned home. He eventually called the next day, but things weren't the same. I can't remember exactly when, but he soon confirmed what my intuition had already let me know: there was someone else. He'd fallen in love with a girl from his school, who went on the mission trip as well. To say I was in a state of shock is an understatement. How did his love for me fade away after one trip? This had to already be in the making.

For the second time in my life, I was depressed. I drove to my parents' house and discussed my heartache with them, which explains how desperate I was, because I never wanted them to see me in a state of despair. However, I was hurting and needed answers. I'm usually pretty good about grooming myself and hygiene, but I remember my sister picking me up around this time, and gently pulling out some lotion for me to put on my face. In that moment it hit me: I was all the way lovesick, to the core of my being. Eventually the situation went from bad to terrible. It wasn't long before he asked her to marry him. The nerve. What was I supposed to do about my feelings? They were all over the place. For a brief moment I contemplated dropping out of school for the semester. I literally couldn't focus. Thank God it was near the end of the year, and I was able to endure.

As pictures from their wedding began to surface on Facebook, my friends told me to stop looking at them. I couldn't help it. Why did he choose her over me? Why not me? Was I not good enough? Was I not pretty enough? I didn't understand. Why did he reject me? It was in these moments that a strong spirit of rejection took over me.

Instead of running to Christ to heal my broken heart, I did the opposite. I was desperate, and eventually found myself aimlessly drifting in the search for love. A man was going to love me, I would make sure of it. I remember one time I kissed three different guys in the span of one week. I'm so ashamed of that. Although I wasn't sexually active, I was emotionally promiscuous. I would find myself in the same cycle: I like a guy. He likes me. We talk for a few months, sometimes exchanging kisses. The end. There was never a real relationship or commitment. This pattern began to do major damage to my self-esteem. I soon came to the conclusion that I was rejected by men.

Slowly but surely, that rejection went from men, to everyone. Once a social butterfly, I hated the idea of meeting new people and making new friendships, because I had a deep fear that I would be rejected. But this was just the beginning. It soon grew like wildfire. If I reached out to you first via Facebook, telephone, etc., and you failed to respond, my mind would automatically think you were mad at me, didn't like me, etc. Can you imagine how exhausting this process can be? Especially since I was tripping off *every little thing*. It was pure torture.

I've been faithfully attending church since I was about 8 years old. It's almost safe to say I've heard about every message there is to be preached. However, I'd never heard anyone speak on the spirit of rejection, until my beautiful Aunt Gayle spoke to the entire church about this spirit, but the entire time I felt as if she was speaking directly to me. Talk about liberating. After years of secretly wondering if something was wrong with me or if I was just overly sensitive, I was able to pinpoint exactly what was happening to me. Now the question was: How do I make it stop?

We're all familiar with the story of Peter denying Jesus in the Bible. Jesus, being omniscient, knew Peter would deny him, so he prayed for him in advance. Jesus prayed that Peter's faith would not fail and he would strengthen the brethren after he was converted (Luke 22:31-32). And it came to pass—Peter denied Jesus not once, but three times.

It's easy for us modern-day Christians to criticize Peter for denying Christ, but I honestly don't know what I would have done if I were in Peter's shoes. In their eyes, they were connecting Peter to a hypocrite, who deserved death. Think of someone in today's society who is deemed insane, a liar, and hypocrite. Now imagine you're being questioned by authorities and the community for being a follower of that individual. What do you do? What do you say when you know they're planning to kill this individual and anyone connected to them? This is what Peter went through, so in his moments of weakness, he denied Christ.

Why did I bring this up? Because, even though Peter denied Christ, in the end, Christ did not reject Peter. In the 21st chapter of John, Jesus asks Peter three times if he loves him. Each time Peter answers "Yes," and Jesus follows up with instructing Peter to feed his sheep. Peter denied Jesus three times, and Jesus followed up with asking Peter if he loved him, as if he was asking for each time Peter denied him. I truly believe he was.

Christ is not like man. He had every right to reject Peter, but he didn't. Instead, he gave Peter a second chance, by allowing him to profess his love for Christ not once but three times. Jesus even gave Peter the sacred job of feeding his sheep, which is basically giving people the gospel. Even after Peter denied Jesus, Christ still accepted him and found him worthy to share the gospel. Amazing!

In the midst of my never-ending, tormenting battle with the spirit of rejection, this revelation of Peter and Christ lifted a huge burden from me. Christ never rejected me. His acceptance eliminated my anxiety and gave me peace that surpassed all understanding. I am not a reject. You are not a reject. Christ has accepted us all and found us worthy of His love.

Eventually, after deleting my ex off Facebook and sending a hateful email, I was able to reconcile with this brother in Christ. I had to believe, that just like God had a plan for him, God also had a plan for me. And although it hurt, I had to let it go. I'm now friends with him and his wife on Facebook. I enjoy seeing pictures of their beautiful family and seeing what God is doing in their ministry. I'd be a fool to shame this man's character and integrity. We both were young and both lacked the wisdom of guarding our hearts.

Prayer for Rejection

Dear God,

You see me. You know me, inside and out, and you have accepted me. Deliver me from the spirit of rejection. Permanently remove tormenting thoughts that cloud my mind. Help me to genuinely love people without fearing they'll fail to do the same. Let your love satisfy me. Let your presence in my life be evident. Let your peace liberate me. Thank you for finding me worthy of your love. Thank you for being the God who sees. I love you.

Amen.

Chapter 2:
Never Pursue a Man

"You are the catch." These are the words my stepfather echoed to me throughout my teenage years, and well into young adulthood. He firmly believed a woman should never chase a man, and with that being said, I wasn't able to receive phone calls from boys or date until I was 17. One of my first dates consisted of myself, my date, and my cousin. Romantic, right? At times I thought my stepfather was being overly strict. However, as I got older and was able to make my own choices, I realized maybe there was a method to his madness.

After experiencing my first heartbreak, it's safe to say I was on a mission to find true love. During that time, I visited my cousin who was attending college in a different state. She was in the gospel choir and invited me to the concert. A few of my college buddies and I used this as an excuse to finally take that road trip we'd been dying for. After arriving, my cousin showed us around campus and took us to the local mall. We ran into a few of her male friends. In typical Nikki style, I found myself attracted to one in particular. I played it cool, but was definitely hoping I'd see him again sometime that weekend. I did. A few times. There was something extremely charming about him. I couldn't deny we had a little chemistry between us. This is why I was a bit shocked he didn't ask for my number as we exchanged goodbyes. No worries. I would find him. And that's exactly what I did.

Thanks to Facebook I was able to locate him immediately and didn't waste time sending him a friend request and initiating a full blown conversation in his inbox. The very next weekend he was in Chicago. It almost pains me to say this, but once again I wasted no time initiating a make out session with him. It's nothing but the grace of God that enabled me to maintain my virginity during this time of extreme emotional promiscuity.

Whatever we had lasted for four years. I say "whatever we had" because it was never an official relationship. I could never get him to commit to me. We had plenty of "DTR" (define the relationship) conversations, but they always resulted in him not feeling "lead" to be in a relationship with me at the time. I can't fail to mention that I was always the one initiating those conversations. However, he did feel lead to spend numerous hours almost every night on the phone with me, kiss me, and I can't forget about that one holiday he spent with me and my family. Does anyone else see anything wrong with this picture?

Sadly, I couldn't see while being in the midst of it, but I knew things weren't adding up. This is why I would "break things off" with him every other season, or give him an ultimatum that always resulted in being an epic fail. Man, love/lust/desperation/thirst/foolishness is blind. Are you ready for the shocker? Not long after whatever we had came to an end, he relocated, and seemingly entered into a relationship immediately. I wasn't crushed, but I must admit I felt some type of way. I was down with him when all he had was a bike and a bus card. I loved him through seasons, and he overlooked my dedication for someone he recently met? I was already done, but that was the nail in the coffin. Clearly God a plan for me, that didn't include him. After four years of hoping one day he'd be ready to commit to me, I had to let him go.

We have ourselves to blame. It takes two. Although I was taught to never pursue a man, I was the one who searched for him on Facebook and sent him a request. I was the one who kissed him first. I initially pursued him, which means I got myself into that four-year period of confusion, heartbreak, and rejection. On numerous occasions I drove hours to visit him in his state. Each and every time, my parents would give me a hard time, saying it wasn't my place as a woman to drive three hours alone to visit a man. In retrospect, I shouldn't have because:

1. He wasn't my man.
2. If he wanted me, he could have come and got me.
3. Number 2 needs to be repeated: *If he wanted me, he would have come and got me.*

When I say if he wanted me, he would have come and got me, I mean that in every single way. He would come to me, instead of allowing me to make those three-hour drives alone. And on top of that, he would have made me his woman, with no questions asked. That's what men do when they want a woman, right? They pursue her.

In my blindness I made excuses for him, but I couldn't ignore the fact that I'd seen how a man pursues a woman he really wants, and it was a beautiful thing to witness. I'd seen men relocate across the country, to be closer to the woman they love. Sounds familiar? Here's why:

Therefore shall a man leave his father and his mother, and shall cleave unto his wife: and they shall be one flesh.

Genesis 2:24

Before I began to date my husband, I reached a really strong and independent place in life. I was excited about my relationship with Christ, my career as a writer, and simply living my life. And it seemed like for the first time ever, I wasn't concerned about dating or any man in particular. It wasn't until my husband came along I was truly able to see that a woman NEVER has to pursue a man. I never had to question when or if he was going to call me, because I was too busy answering his phone calls. I never wondered when would be the next time I'd see him, because he'd plan our next date as we said our goodbyes from the date we were currently on. He only wanted me and he made that extremely clear. There were never any blurred lines. He was chasing after me, making it clear that I was a prize worth chasing.

Sometimes I wish I could go back to my teenage years and start over. While I never flat out pursued a guy, I had thirsty tendencies, which wasn't any better. Being thirsty didn't get me anywhere far, because God's word still proved to be true:

He who finds a wife, finds a good thing and obtains favor from The Lord.

Proverbs 18:22

It's *he* who finds a wife, not *she* who finds a husband. My dear sisters, allow him to pursue you. It's a beautiful feeling to know you were his most prized possession, worth pursuing. Are you currently pursuing a guy? *Stop* it. Unsure? Here's how to know if you're doing the pursuing:

- You usually call or text him first
- You create little moments for you two to be together a.k.a. fake dates

- Most of the time you're the one driving to his house or meeting him somewhere (a man pursuing you will pick you up, especially if he has a car)
- You're unsure about the status of your "relationship"
- You're the one who initiates the "define the relationship" conversations

I hate to say it, but I've been there, done that, wrote the book (literally), and bought the t-shirt. It leads to nothing but self-destruction and a motherlode of rejection issues that will spiral out of control if not dealt with immediately.

Can I share a secret with you? Most of the men I dealt with in the past, reached out to congratulate me on my engagement and jumping the broom. I thought it was cool and honorable of them to do that. However, the brother I'm speaking of above, never said anything to this day. It's almost like he has chosen to ignore this blissful time in my life. Or maybe he truly doesn't care. My friends believe he realizes he lost a good woman. I think I agree, and if that's the case, I'm mad at myself for enduring a pseudo relationship for four years. Why did I partially take blame for him rejecting me? Why didn't I know I was enough? Thank God for restoring the years and time I wasted, and allowing me to experience what it really feels like to be wildly pursued. It. Feels. GOOD.

I was worth so much more. YOU ARE WORTH SO MUCH MORE. The Bible says we're fearfully and wonderfully made (Psalms 139:14). Walk in that truth and allow him to pursue you. You are the prize.

A Prayer for Self-Esteem

Dear God,

Thank you for calling me by name. Thank you for redeeming me. Thank you for allowing me to belong to you (Isaiah 43:1). God you said I am fearfully and wonderfully made. (Psalm 139:14) Help me to truly believe that. Your word says, "He who finds a wife, finds a good thing." (Proverbs 18:22) If it's in your will for me to be a wife, let me find peace in knowing my husband will find me. Allow me to be pursued. I am a virtuous woman and my worth is far above rubies (Proverbs 31:10). I am the prize.

Amen.

Chapter 3:
Guard Your Heart

It really bothers me when people give out terrible advice that consists of the famous saying, "Follow your heart." It's extra annoying when Christians suggest this. Why?

The heart is deceitful above all things, and desperately wicked: who can know it?

Jeremiah 17:9

This verse teaches us two things about the heart: it is deceitful and desperately wicked. If that's the case, why do we grant our hearts permission to govern our lives? Ever heard the saying, "Never make a permanent decision based on temporary feelings"? This is because the heart can be offended one second, and over it the next. Almost like how we can be in "love" with a man one day, and totally done the next, simply because we hate the way he chews his food. I can't tell you how many men I've been "in love" with, only to discover that it wasn't love after all. What happened? I had a change of (you guessed it) *heart.*

This is why it's imperative that we constantly check our hearts. Especially women. It can be second nature for a woman to wear her heart on her sleeve. We're natural caregivers and lovers. Call me biased, but a woman's touch makes everything better. However, we have to be extremely careful. Only one man is deserving of your good loving and affection, and that's your husband. I learned the hard way. I cringe when I think about all of the home cooked meals I made for the men I was *hoping* to one day be my husband. Who knows what they've done with the secrets I shared with them from my heart, if they even remember or were truly paying attention. Oh how desperate the heart is for attention and affection, when in actuality it needs to be guarded, which leads me to my point: *Guard your heart.*

Watch over your heart with all diligence, for from it flows the springs of life.

Proverbs 4:23

I'll never forget the moment this scripture actually began to mean something to me. After years of pursuing men, dealing with rejection, and being an emotional wreck, the Lord gently informed me that I wasn't guarding my heart. It's a shame to think about how many years I wasted mishandling my love life, when God's word had provided me with clear instructions. Not only does the scripture inform us to guard our heart, but it adds "with all diligence." This isn't something to be taken lightly. Ever wondered why a woman chooses to stay in an abusive relationship? Or how people find themselves in silly love triangles? Why won't they just leave? It's easier said than done. The heart is tricky. Common sense isn't common when the heart is involved. People become extremely irrational when it comes to matters of the heart. This is why it *must* be guarded. It isn't an option.

Recently a friend asked me, how did I guard my heart without putting up walls? It wasn't easy, but I reached a point where my heart was literally tired. It could only take so much rejection, neglect, and abuse, before it began to cry out for true redemption. Finally, after years of doing things my way, I was ready to surrender my love life to God. Here are a few things that helped me along the way:

I ended all of my online dating subscriptions.

I completely understand that online dating will be the source as to how some people will find their mate. However, as for me, God clearly told me to cancel my memberships. In retrospect, now I know why: I wasn't going to meet my future husband on any of those sites, and me logging on every few days to discover only the weirdos had taken an interest in me was adding to my rejection. Nope. It wasn't for me.

I ruled out any potentials.

What about him? Or him? Could he be my husband? Those "should've, could've, would'ves" will drive you crazy. What messes us up in the head is how we think, or who we think, it should be. If he wasn't actively pursuing me, I made the fairytale come to an end, immediately. I was waiting for my real love. As Lauryn Hill said, "Fantasy is what people want, but reality is what they need."

I learned how to enjoy Nikki.

I started going to the movies alone, and I actually enjoyed it. I would take a walk every Sunday in my neighborhood, and began my own tradition of praying every Sunday night, asking God to cover and prepare me for the week ahead. During this time I also began to develop my skills and career as a writer. I put all of my extra time into my blog, NikkiAndTheCity.com, and began to see results. I was intentional about spending time with loved ones, and made sure my relationship with God was intact.

I got to a point where I was genuinely enjoying life. Although I hated my job, I was going to church, working out, and my blog was taking off. I was so deep into my routine and my heart was so guarded, that when I first noticed my husband, Steve, my initial reaction was to make it go away. What's "it"? Any feelings of attraction to him. It was my desire to stay focused and not allow my heart to get wrapped up in another pointless crush. I'll never forget a prayer my aunt prayed for me when I was in my early 20s:

"Father, I pray Nikki gives her heart to you, and you give it to the man you have for her." That has always stuck with me.

I can't tell you how many times I prayed for the feelings I had for my husband to go away. They never did. However, the best thing about guarding your heart is it keeps you from doing the most. I wasn't on Stevie's Facebook page liking all his pictures, or texting him all the time. I actually shied away from him. I gave the entire matter to God, and trusted that if Stevie was for me, God would allow him to come to me. That's exactly what happened. My beautiful man came to me.

I must admit, the early stages of us dating were super scary for me. I'd grown accustomed to guarding my heart and was a bit paranoid about letting my walls down. For a brief moment I thought about running away from Stevie and informed my sister that I was going to break up with him. It was too good to be true and I was scared. Thank God I didn't break up with him. Instead, I fasted for an entire day, seeking the Lord about our relationship. I didn't take any phone calls and refrained from social media. I needed the Lord to ensure me that it was okay to let my guard down. Taking that day to pray and be quiet before the Lord was the best thing ever for me, and the worst for Stevie. He went crazy without me. That day confirmed that we were meant to be together.

Also, I later found out at my bridal shower that my day of fasting was the same day Stevie realized he couldn't live without me. We started dating, and six months later he asked me to marry him. What's crazy is, at first it was hard for me to go a day without speaking to Stevie. We spoke *every* day. I thought if I messed up the flow, I was risking him forgetting about me, or realizing he doesn't need to talk to me every day. Thank God I was able to sacrifice that one day. In return, God has given me a lifetime with the man He had for me.

So, to answer the question, how do you guard your heart, without putting up walls? You give your heart *completely* to God and let *Him* do the guarding. You walk softly before the Lord and listen to His voice. If He tells you to end a relationship, end it. Obedience is better than sacrifice.

Seek the face of the Lord about your love life and be open to what He has to say. I dreaded praying the following prayer: "Lord, am I supposed to get married one day or remain single the rest of my life?"

Trust me, I wasn't being a brat when I prayed that prayer. I needed answers, because some women will never get married. I needed God to let me know which path He had for me, so I could finally find rest. I was relieved when He told me, "It's not your time, yet."

Often we find ourselves confused about what God is doing in our life, but newsflash: *God is always speaking.* We just have to seek His face. Get it? Guarding your heart protects you from so much unnecessary drama and heartache. It's also the perfect way to preserve your heart for the spouse God may have for you. Live. Laugh. Love. And don't forget to guard that heart.

A Prayer to Guard Your Heart

Dear God,

Regardless of what society may say, I acknowledge that my heart is deceitful and wicked (Jeremiah 17:9). I need your instruction on how to guard it. God, help me find the perfect balance. Lord, I give you my entire heart and trust you will give it to the man you may have for me. In the meantime, help me to be anxious for nothing. May my heart be still and find solitude in you.

Amen.

Chapter 4:
What to Do While You're Single

When I was a lonely, single, 20-year-old, my mentor told me to plan my wedding. And guess what? That's exactly what I did. In retrospect, that was the worst advice to give a single woman. There I was planning my wedding, that wouldn't occur until a whole 10 years later. What a waste. Thank God before I met my husband I'd finally reached a place of being content in my singleness. If I could relive my single days again, here's a list of things I'd do differently:

School

I am a first-generation college student, which means neither one of my parents attended college. I never thought I'd receive my bachelor's degree, so quite naturally grad school wasn't an option for me, until it was. In retrospect, I have no idea why I never seriously pursued grad school. Of course the thought of taking the GRE terrified me, but I'd purchased a few used books to help me study for it, even though I never took it. Instead, I took the first job that was offered to me after I completed an internship in Mississippi and moved back to Chicago. God has been good to me in my career choice, but sometimes I wish I'd made time for another degree.

Entrepreneurship

I guess you can call me a business woman. This is solely based on all of the seminars and conferences I attended within the past five years, along with the experience that comes along with building a brand. When I think about all the success I've had with my blog, NikkiAndTheCity.com, I'm always amazed at how I was able to build something out of *nothing*. Of course all of the credit and glory goes to God. I'm beyond grateful.

However, sometimes I can't help but lament over how much time I wasted prior to getting married. I was 30 years old when I said I do. What was I doing with my free time in my 20s? I wish I had a solid answer for you, but I don't. It hurts me to say most of my time was spent on men who were clearly *not* my husband. If only I could have those evenings and weekends back. My career would be so much farther along than it is now. Oh well, you live and you learn.

Family

I'm the poster child for blended families. Literally. I have three brothers and three sisters, but I'm my parents' only child together. Go figure. Needless to say I have *plenty* of family. I wish I would have been more intentional about cultivating those relationships. Now that I'm married I have *more* family, almost too much to handle. I feel bad about not being able to give people the proper one-on-one time that's needed to grow a healthy relationship. Being single can feel lonely at times, but think about those who are dying to spend time with you. Spend a day thrifting with your grandmother. Check out an NBA game with your father and brother. Have a sleepover with your little

Chapter 5:
Purity is Possible

I'd like to inform you that I was a 30-year-old virgin. While this may be shocking for some, I know a lot of women who were in the same boat with me. I struggled with sharing my story, because of people's doubt and disbelief. Then it dawned on me that I'd be remiss not to give all the glory to God for what He did in my sex life, not me. So, here it is.

My family has always called me "scary" and it's semi-true.

"What was that noise?"

"Why is that man standing over there?"

I was known for being overly cautious. I guess my fearful ways spilled over into the bedroom, because the thought of having sex scared the crap out of me. See, if you think I remained a virgin because I'm super holy, you're completely wrong. I was scared until the age of 15, when I started dating a guy I really liked. It wasn't long before he began to put pressure on me to have sex. This is when I really began to contemplate doing it. I still don't know if my stepfather's intuition informed him of what was happening, or if he found a note in my room. I believe it to be the latter. All I know is my stepfather took me out to the movies and asked a million questions about this situation.

Let's not get it twisted; he wasn't trying to badger me. In fact, he was schooling me on how to handle this immature high school situation, because we both knew I really didn't want to have sex with my boyfriend, but I didn't want to lose him either. I took his advice, informing my boyfriend that I was worth the wait. Well, apparently he didn't think so and we broke up. I lost my *boy*friend, but I kept something so precious that was only worth giving to a *man*, better known as my husband: my virginity.

Two years later at 17, God got a hold of my heart and I completely gave my life to Christ. I realized I couldn't do anything outside of God and without Him my life was pointless (John 15:5). Pretty deep for a 17-year-old, right? Now, I wasn't perfect. I dated my fair share of guys and kissed a bunch of frogs.

However, I never compromised my Christianity by having sex before marriage. I remember when a family member thought they knew about me sleeping with one of their friend's sons. There was another situation when a guy I was dating lied, saying we slept together. And of course there are the smart comments people would make every blue moon about me not being a virgin. I've ignored them, but let's be clear: I heard them loud and clear. But I'll address that later.

We're all grown here, right? I hope so. Did you know when you have sex with someone the two of you become one?

For this reason a man will leave his father and mother and be united to his wife, and the two will become one flesh.

Ephesians 5:31

When you become one with someone, it's *hard* to let them go. That's because your body was never meant to become one with a random person or multiple people in the first place. Sex is a beautiful thing. However, it's so beautiful and precious that God put a fence around it to protect it. That fence is marriage. Also, did you know that sexual immorality is the only sin that is referenced to as "sinning against your own body"?

Flee from sexual immorality. All other sins a person commit are outside the body, but whoever sins sexually, sins against their own body.

1 Corinthians 6:18

Who really wants to sin against their own body? I'm so thankful that these were the type of conversations and Bible studies I had the privilege to be involved in, which encouraged me to abstain from sex before marriage. A few years ago, I ran into the ex-boyfriend from high school who was pressuring me to have sex. He saw me crossing the street and honked to get my attention. We exchanged a few words and that was that. As I laid in bed later on that evening, I couldn't help but to feel extremely grateful to God. What if I had given in and allowed him to take my virginity, only to randomly run into him on the streets years later? No ma'am. I totally dodged a bullet.

But when I think things over, it would have been like that for *every* relationship I was in, with the exception of my fiancé. Let's face it, none of those relationships were leading to marriage. They all resulted in me being insecure, feeling rejected, and heartbroken. I'm almost sure the pain would have been worse, if I'd given myself to them physically. Talk about an ungodly soul tie for real. It's funny how society tries to flip the script and make it seem like if you're not having sex before marriage, you're being uptight and ridiculous.

Listen, God knows what He is doing. He's sparing us

from a whole lot of unnecessary drama: single parenting, STDs, broken hearts, etc. However, we're only human and I'm aware that this type of drama unfortunately occurs in marriages sometimes. We never understand why, especially when people commit their life to someone before God, family, and friends. All we can do is pray and trust God's heart. Now, I'm no angel and I don't want you to think it was easy not to have sex. It was *hard*. I remember praying to God, "I'm getting too old not to be sexually active. A sister has needs." As our wedding date approached, I felt like I could see the light at the end of the tunnel. And the best part was, I knew I would be giving my husband a gift no man had ever gotten from me. Take my word—it was so worth the wait.

Was our wedding night physically magical? Of course not. It takes time. However, it was magical in the sense that we have the rest of our lives to love on each other, and we were just getting started. Purity is possible. It amazes me at how many people believe it's impossible to abstain from sex before marriage.

Remaining pure can't be done in your own strength. You must lean solely on the power of God. He will keep you, if you want to be kept. I'm a living witness. Whether you're a virgin or born-again virgin, walk in the grace God has given you. Don't be ashamed of your powerful testimony. Also, don't concern yourself with who believes you. All you can do is give all the glory right back to God. It may seem impossible to remain a virgin in a sex-driven culture, but my God is greater. Purity is possible, and you are so worth the wait.

A Prayer for Purity

Dear God,
 As a single woman, my body belongs to you. Please forgive me for the times I've been tempted to think otherwise. Because I can do

all things through you who gives me strength, I can abstain from having sex until I am a married woman. Create in me a clean heart and renew within me a right spirit. Please shield me from being influenced by society's promiscuity. May I hunger for modesty and purity. May I never be ashamed to uphold a holy standard. I pray this for my sisters and brothers as well. Purity is possible.

Amen.

Chapter 6:
When True Love Finds You

If it's in God's will for you to be married one day, stress not, true love *will* find you. I'll never forget my initial response to my husband's first attempt at pursuing me: I prayed for him to go away.

Here's why: I've never been the type of woman who struggled with loving a man. As a matter of fact, my struggle was the exact opposite. I yearned to love a man. Cook his dinner. Kiss his lips. Pray for him. Pray with him. Love him. I wanted to be a wife; however, I knew if I wasn't careful I'd give him all of me, before it was time. Besides, I'd been there before. I've played the role of a "wife" when I wasn't even a girlfriend. Shame on me. There's something so beautiful about what happens when a man opens up more layers to a woman that she never knew were there before. However, that magic must be protected and kept only for her husband. This is why I was praying for the feelings I had for Stevie to go away, because if I would have let myself go without the Lord's approval, it would have been awful. And to be honest, I didn't have time to endure another heartbreak or pointless relationship. I had finally reached a place in life where I was content being single, and the powerful force I felt towards Stevie was a direct threat to the victory I'd obtained thus far. I was terrified.

This may sound strange, but I felt Steve coming. It's hard to explain, but when that season of love for me arrived, it was almost like my husband and I became magnets. We were drawn to each other. I would go to his Facebook page all the time, extremely careful *not* to hit the "like" button on anything. I had no idea he was doing the exact same thing. I had to gain control of my heart ASAP, because I was falling at an unnatural, dangerously fast speed. I honestly had a love for my husband *before* he pursued me. In retrospect, I now believe God had given me a heart specifically for Stevie, because he was going to be my husband. But before there was any hint of us being together I asked God to guard my heart. I begged him to take away the feelings I had for Steve, if he wasn't going to be my husband. He answered my prayer by *never* taking those feelings away. Now that I'm his wife, I completely understand why God allowed those feelings to remain.

The Month I Didn't Talk to Men

Let me first start out by saying I'm not one of those Christians who claim to hear from God all the time. To be honest, God has never audibly spoke to me, but I always know when He's speaking to my spirit. It was February 2013. I can't remember where I was, or what I was doing. I suddenly had what I considered a regular thought: "Don't talk to any men for an entire month." Where did that thought come from? I immediately dismissed it. A few days later the same thought came to me, but this time it was different: "You shouldn't be talking to any men this month." This time I knew this was indeed the Lord speaking to me, but there was one major problem that was quite confusing: *I already wasn't talking to any men.* I didn't have a boyfriend, boo, or random. There was NO ONE. Who was I supposed to not talk to? Nevertheless, I concluded with only speaking to the men in my family during what I was now calling a "man fast." If I only knew what the next 30 days had in store for me. I seriously cannot make this stuff up. A different man reached out to me almost *every day* during my 30-day man fast. I would literally go to work and show a new message to my roommate and co-worker. They were aware of my man fast and couldn't believe what was happening as well. It wasn't difficult not talking to these men, although I did wonder about their intentions. It became clear that God was doing something, which encouraged me to simply be obedient:

Guard thy heart with all diligence; for out of it are the issues of life.
Proverbs 4:23

Boy oh boy, I am a bit too familiar with this scripture. This had become my go-to scripture whenever I became frustrated with dating. Realizing I'm a sucker for love, I saw exactly why the Lord informed me to refrain from talking to men during that time. Can you imagine my heart being pulled in a million directions? I would have been entertaining a plethora of men, who clearly were not my future husband. I guess the Lord decided to help me guard my heart, since I wasn't exactly a pro at it. Isn't He such a great Father?

February 2013 was spent not talking to any men, in obedience to God. By the time February 2014 arrived, I was engaged. In February 2015, I celebrated my first Valentine's Day as a married woman. Do you see the pattern? Obedience is always better. In April 2013 my soon-to-be husband started reaching out to me. Sometimes I wonder where I would be if I had decided to ignore the nudge of God. I can't imagine missing out on the awesome blessing of marrying Mr. Stephen. Seriously, I can go on and on for days about how amazing my man is. But the best part is, I submitted myself to God, and allowed HIM (and only him) to write my love story.

Sisters…Has God called you to give up something or someone? DO. IT. My former pastor always says God isn't trying to take something from you, He's trying to give something to you. God wasn't trying to take me away from men; he was trying to prepare me for my soon to be, only husband. Get it? Good. Now completely trust the Father. P.S. I'm always receiving emails from sisters inquiring about the month I didn't talk to men. I'm pleased to announce there is now a devotional entitled "The 30-Day Man Fast." Please visit www.NikkiCarpenter.com for more information.

A Prayer to Wait for True Love

Dear God,

Your word tells me not to awaken love before its time (Song of Solomon 8:4). Please help me to take heed. If it is indeed in your will for me to be a wife one day, you know exactly where my future husband is, you know exactly where I am, and you know exactly when our paths will cross. Help me to wait on you and not settle out of desperation. Also, help me to be ready for my moment for love. I wait on you.

Amen.

Chapter 7:
My Future Husband Was Already Married

Man makes plans. God laughs. I can't tell you how many times I thought I knew who my future husband would be. I heard this saying when I was single and found it to be true: "It's the person you least expect it to be." It sure was, because my future husband was already married. After experiencing my first heartbreak, I was sure I'd meet my husband at college. It just made sense. It didn't bother me that I attended a predominantly White institution. If God didn't plan on me marrying a brother, I had no problem being down with the swirl. Well, after three years of a few crushes and almost-but-not-really relationships, I walked away with a degree, but no husband. Ugh. After graduation I headed to Jackson, Mississippi for a year-long internship. Maybe my future husband was a fine Southern man with hospitality and charm.

After one year of random dates, a major crush, and a failed relationship, I came back to Chicago single as a dollar bill. There was a guy I could've gotten serious with in Jackson; however, I never had peace about that situation. I would soon learn why. After getting settled back in Chicago, finding a job, and an apartment, I went on a few dates here and there, but it was never anything serious. This bothered me. I was over 25 and my dating life was non-existent. I didn't even have any prospects, besides my ongoing fantasy of marrying HuffPost Live's Marc Lamont Hill. To make matters worse, it seemed like everyone around me was getting married and starting their lives.

I couldn't understand it. I had a degree, a job, a car, my own place, and no kids. I went from wondering what was wrong with these men out here, to wondering what was wrong with *me*, which is a dangerous place to be. If it wasn't for my relationship with God, I would've remained in a place of depression and rejection. I'm in no way saying one day I woke up and felt completely satisfied with my single status. Not at all. There was a lot of back and forth going on. A lot of tears, plenty of conversations with God, and two dreams that I'll never forget that I know without a shadow of doubt was God letting me know it wasn't my time…yet.

So, eventually I came to a place of just doing me and being intentional about enjoying life as a single woman. Meanwhile, on a few occasions my best friend Briana told me to pray for a friend of hers who was battling cancer. I'd never met her, but knew of her husband Stephen. Every now and then I'd ask Briana about her friend's health and was saddened to hear about her passing away. I felt so sad for Stephen. He was an extremely young widow. I couldn't imagine what he was feeling, so I gave my condolences and made sure to keep him in my prayers.

Months passed, and the guy from Mississippi began to come on to me really strong. I thought to myself, "Why not?" I knew he loved me and would treat me like a queen. We had a phone conversation that resulted in us giving our relationship another chance, but taking it slow. After I hung up the phone, I felt extremely uneasy. It may seem weird, but I felt like I was cheating on Steve. It's hard to explain. I've never heard the voice of God audibly, but I heard in my spirit that if I opened up the door with this guy in Mississippi, I would miss out on my opportunity with Steve. Huh? Where did that come from?

I knew I had to be tripping, so I immediately dismissed that thought. However, a few days passed and nothing changed. I still felt uneasy about starting a romantic relationship with the guy in Mississippi. Maybe this was God telling me something, so I figured it was safer for me to be obedient than sorry. I told the guy in Mississippi that I didn't have a peace about us and had to obey the voice of the Lord. It didn't go over too easy for both of us. I'm convinced he thought I'd lost my mind. On the other hand, I was ending a relationship to be with a man who showed *zero* interest in me, and on top of all that, had recently lost his wife. For a moment I thought I'd lost my mind as well, until God's will began to beautifully manifest itself.

It started with a few glances, and I even believe we locked eyes a few times. Was Stevie staring at me? This is what would take place whenever I saw Stevie. It felt good and bad at the same time: "I couldn't like a man who lost his wife. It wasn't right. And besides, he wasn't even thinking of me. Or was he? Forget it. Forget everything." These were the thoughts running through my head and since I don't believe in a woman pursuing a man, all I could do was wait. And then it happened.

Stevie was having a concert for his "EUROCLYDON" album and asked if I could be on his marketing team. Of course I could! Stevie went from texting me all day, every day, to finally calling me one Monday evening. Stevie says after that 15-minute phone call, he needed more of me in his life. We talked every day and night, for hours and hours. It was obvious we were falling in love with each other, but I never said a word. I

Chapter 8:
When Christian Men Break Your Heart

I couldn't believe it happened to me. My first heartbreak came from a man of God. He was actually the son of a preacher, with aspirations to lead his own flock one day. Out of all the silly, mediocre relationships I'd been in that amounted to nothing, I just knew I hit the jackpot when I started dating my man of God. I just knew we'd get married and live happily ever after. Why? Because he was a Christian man. He wouldn't leave me. He wouldn't break my heart.

After all was said and done, I couldn't decide what hurt the most: the fact that he chose another woman over me, or the fact that a man of God actually broke my heart. As I write this post, I'm struggling with what *not* to say, but it must be said. Some (a huge emphasis on some) Christian men have done a terrible job on helping guard the hearts of their sisters in the church. I've seen it up close and personal. I've experienced it. I've seen men practically go through entire congregations and friendship circles, in an effort to find their wife. In some cases I've seen men go so far as to proposing to a woman, having her uproot her entire life to be with him, only to say, "Oops, God said you're not the one."

"God said."

Now let's repeat it in the form of a question: "God said?" I too, was hit with the "God said you're not my wife" line. It even happened during the middle of a date. That line always confused me, because if these men were listening to God to hear him say I wasn't the one, then how come they didn't hear God tell them not to approach me in the first place? Unsolved mysteries, right? Before you guys begin to label me as a "Bitter Christian Woman," please believe I'm not. I'm now married to the man of my dreams. God knows I'm not trying to place all the blame on men, but it took me being pursued by my husband, to realize the huge responsibility men in the church have. The ball is *always* in their court:

He who finds a wife finds a good thing and obtains favor from the Lord.

Proverbs 18:22

He who finds a wife. Not *she* who finds a husband. At times, this was the hardest part about being single. I had to wait for my husband to find me. I don't believe in women pursuing men, so when I would be approached by Christian men, I took it extremely seriously. Why? I assumed these men were looking for their wife and had taken the time to talk to God about me, before their initial approach.

Boy was I wrong, on too many occasions. And because the Bible says we are fearfully and wonderfully made, and made in the image of God, I assumed Christian men had this in mind when approaching women in the church. Why was I so naive?

After two heartbreaks and a few disappointments along my love life journey, I came to the conclusion that I

Chapter 9:
How to Know Who Your Husband Is

Nine times out of ten, you have a clear idea of who your husband *isn't*. I'm 100 percent sure of this. How? The Bible says: "My sheep hear my voice, and I know them, and they follow me" (John 10:27).

Your Husband is Not Someone Else's Husband

This may be obvious to some of you, but 20-year-old Nikki struggled with this. I was a student at the local community college. He was an advisor and favored a celebrity who was extremely successful and popular at that time. I can't remember how our conversation transitioned from studies to flirting, but it did, quickly. I knew our texting and emailing was wrong, but I couldn't force myself to stop. Why? I'd convinced myself he was going to get a divorce, so it was okay. Even when I asked him if he'd planned to get a divorce and he said "No," I still couldn't let go. Although we texted and emailed a lot, we'd never seen each other outside the school. One night he asked me to meet him. We met in the parking lot of a mall nearby. While we chatted in his car, his wife believed he'd made a quick run to the store. Terrible. And then it happened. We kissed. It wasn't a simple peck. It was a French/tongue/inappropriate kiss.

As I drove home I was sure God was going to cause me to get in a major accident, due to the sin I just committed. Although we didn't have sex, we'd committed adultery. I was extremely mad at myself. When did I become that woman? I reached a new low in life. To make matters worse, I was 20 years old at the time, and he was 31. Not only did he have a wife at home, but she'd recently given birth to a baby girl. I was done. It wasn't worth it. I couldn't fool God. I knew he wasn't getting a divorce and even if he was, he was still married and belonged to his wife:

Let every man have his own wife, and let every woman have her own husband.

1 Corinthians 7:2

My knowledge was against me. I knew better, so I cut it off. Besides, I wanted my own husband and the kiss we shared wasn't that good anyway. In addition to the married man, there were so many single guys I knew for a fact were *not* my husband, but I still entertained them out of boredom or fear of being lonely. On a few occasions the men the Lord told me to leave alone ended up moving out of town. Each time it happened I knew it was the Lord drastically separating me from those men, since my disobedience had prohibited me from letting them go.

Even as I write this, I can't help but acknowledge how much mercy the Father showed me. He could have allowed me to fulfill the lusts of my flesh, since I knew His voice, but blocked it out in an effort to have a man. Age and wisdom is teaching me not to ignore God's voice. It is said, "Today if you hear his voice, do not harden your hearts, as when they provoked me" (Hebrews 3:15). Obedience is always better. Always. (1 Samuel 15:22) If you're in a relationship or situation with a man who you know for a fact God has said to not entertain, let it go. Immediately. It is impossible to manipulate a blessing from God. Trust me, I've tried.

He lived in California and I was living in Chicago. We met on Facebook. Maybe that should have been my red flag? However, it was hard to pass up a Black Christian man who graduated from an HBCU for undergrad, was on their way to an Ivy League school, and who was totally into me. Why wouldn't God allow him to be my husband? He even had a love for Black history, which was the cherry on top. I decided he'd be "the one," and entered into a strange relationship with him.

Everything became extremely intense, way too fast. He referred to me as his wife, and one time we even quoted "vows" on the phone to each other. (Sidenote: I don't recommend any woman ever share vows with a man, unless you're at the altar getting married. Why? The intensity of what he promised and how he vowed to love me, most definitely made me want him sexually, which could have been a disastrous problem if we didn't live thousands of miles away from one another.) We would spend hours upon hours on the phone, and when we'd hang up, I'd receive a text from him saying "I miss you." It seemed a little possessive and romantic, at the same time. He really impressed me when he'd analyze my writings. I found it quite lovely that a man would take time to study and understand the makings of me. We hadn't met face to face, but I was almost sure I'd found love.

Everything changed the weekend he came to visit me in Chicago. It wasn't his looks. He was indeed who he said he was on Facebook. It was his personality. Things I found hilarious were not funny to him, at all. He was also slightly socially awkward, which was hard for me, because I'm definitely an extroverted social butterfly. I spent the entire weekend annoyed, counting down the minutes until his flight departed. Needless to say, I broke up with him on his last day in town. My friends couldn't believe I made him fly all the way to Chicago, just to break up with him. Those were not my intentions. However, I've never been one to successfully camouflage how I feel or pretend to be interested. I saw no future with him and had no trouble letting it go, so I thought. I knew there would be no future for our relationship: however, every now and then I'd seriously consider dating him. I honestly can't remember what I was thinking. I must have desperately believed God would see how good he was for me on paper, and make us compatible for one another.

After a few years of playing merry-go-round, he made his last strong push to make me his woman, and I was giving in. Then something totally unexpected happened. During his brief weekend in Chicago, he'd met a few of my close friends, including a close friend who was more like a sister. She'd relocated to the East Coast and he was aware, thanks to Facebook. He was making a quick trip to her city and briefly mentioned her to me in conversation. I didn't think anything of it.

The next time we talked he started off the conversation by saying how beautiful of a woman she was and some other inappropriate comments, especially since he was "pursuing" me at the moment. And then he dropped the bomb on me. They'd met up during his visit, and the ultimate "no-no" happened—they'd kissed. I'm no fool. It didn't take me long to know this was the Lord's way of confirming to me for the last time that he was not the one for me. I wasn't even mad, as much as I was hurt. I felt semi-betrayed by my friend, who's more like a sister to me, but she was at a vulnerable place in her life at the time.

However, since neither one of us had deep feelings for him, it didn't affect our sisterhood. She informed him that she would no longer be in communication with him, which resulted in him deleting me from Facebook. He also sent me a round of text messages saying how he couldn't believe I was standing in the way of him possibly finding true love, and he couldn't understand why, since all I did was play games with him in the first place. We went back and forth for a while, but I honestly didn't have the energy or passion to prove my point to him. If he couldn't see how pathetic it was of him to pursue a close friend of mine while he was pursuing me, then he wasn't the man for me. Besides, he was right about one thing: I was indeed playing a game with him. I knew years ago he wasn't the one for me, but disobedience and desperation caused me to slightly always leave that door open. It wasn't worth it anymore. He went along his merry way, and I completely shut the door once and for all.

A couple years later, I was on set shooting a show for the TLC network with Steve, who was my fiancé at the time. We were filming a show that highlighted our decision to wait for marriage to have sex. We were six weeks away from our wedding and life was good. I have an iPhone, which allows you to send messages to anyone else with an iPhone through their iCloud account. I received a message that read: "You sure?" It was him.

He may not have wrote much, but he wrote more than he ever should have. I knew exactly what he was hinting at. He was asking me if I was sure about getting married. The nerve of him, right? I showed Steve the message. We laughed it off and I simply responded "Sure about what?" I was going to make him say what he was trying to allude to, instead of shrinking behind a forward, yet vague message. To this day he has never replied to the conversation he initiated. Meanwhile, to answer his question, I've never been so sure about anything in my life. Steve will forever be the best thing that's ever happened to me. Period. It's impossible to manipulate a blessing from God. And if it was possible, I wouldn't want it. I had finally reached a place in my singleness of wanting who God wanted for me. The mind games weren't worth it anymore. There's a peace that comes with fully trusting

God with your life, which includes your love life as well.

Sisters, I can't explain to you the way it feels to be beautifully pursued by the man God has for you. It feels like after years of wondering and waiting, God has finally said...yes. Are you struggling trying to decipher if the man you're entertaining is the one for you? Here are six signs:

Six Signs He's the One

1. He's dating you with a purpose.

What do men mean when they say "Oh, we're just hanging out"? Or how about "We're getting to know each other to see where it goes"? Okay, you can do that as friends, but if you're going to date, do it with a purpose. Is marriage your goal? If not, time is being wasted and who really has time for that?

2. Your relationship is exclusive.

Are people really okay with dating multiple people at a time? Sounds pretty dumb to me. How can you fully get to know a potential life partner, if your time and attention is divided? No ma'am, your relationship needs to be exclusive. If he wants you, he wants only you. That's it, that's all.

3. Family is a priority.

Is he excited about taking you around his family? He should be. When a man finds a good woman, he wants to show you off to all of his family and friends. The most important people in his life *must* meet the most important woman in his life. Also, the same applies for your family. He should want to see the foundation that helped shape and make you the woman you are today.

4. He encourages transparency in your relationship.

There were so many things I was embarrassed and ashamed of, that I would try to hide from Steve. It was so

Chapter 10:
Let God Write Your Love Story

I remember the first time I'd heard the saying, "Let God write your love story." The thought of me doing just that (for once in my life) lifted a huge burden from me. What if I let go of the picture in my head of how it was "supposed" to be, and trust God? What if I didn't allow society's timing of what age I should be married stress me out? What if I made an intentional decision to live up to God's standard and not my own plans for my life? What if?

Unfortunately, me allowing God to write my love story consisted of me constantly going back and forth between His will and mine. I had seasons where I was completely fine being single. However, I also had seasons where I would cry myself to sleep, because I felt lonely and yearned for nothing more than to be married. If I only knew what God was preparing for me behind the scenes.

In December 2012, I was sitting in my living room while my stylist was braiding my hair. I received a call from my mom. I could tell by the tone of her voice she had something important to tell me. She had just left a Christmas party, and while she was there a woman approached her and began to speak into my mom's life. Here's where it gets juicy.

The woman asked my mom if she had a daughter. My mother replied, "Yes." The woman went on to say the following: "Your daughter is not rejected. She could have been married a few times, but God is protecting her. Men see her and find her to be beautiful, but aren't approaching her because God isn't letting them. He put a fence around her, because He already has someone for her. He's a unique man, and he's coming. And when she gets married, she won't have to worry about how the wedding will be paid for."

Whoa.

First let me say, I'm not one to seek out prophets to find out what God is doing in my own life. Experience has taught me to seek God for myself. He's always speaking. However, God was definitely using this woman to speak to me. While I was single people assumed I was going out on plenty of dates, but the truth is I spent a great deal of energy wondering why men weren't asking me out. I definitely struggled with rejection and wondered if men were attracted to me. There were so many things I didn't understand. I had so many questions and in that moment God saw fit to answer me. For once, it all made sense. God was protecting me and I was willing to wait, no matter how long it would take. Steve came into my life four months later.

The Proposal

I thought I was going to a special ESSENCE magazine event in Chicago, with actress Nia Long. My friend Briana knows I love me some Nia Long and had this "event" date on the calendar for months—January 4, 2014. I made sure to do my best makeup and dress up for

Made in the USA
Charleston, SC
05 August 2015